From the Editor

Thank you for your recent Kindle purchase. Here at the Quote Foundry, we have hand picked the most inspiring quotes on leadership from the thousands of quotes we could have chosen. We have sifted through the dirt and left you with diamonds, from some of the most inspiring people in modern history and those we will look to for inspiration in the decades to come.

We hope that this book will give you inspiration, confidence and vision to lead your team, or yourself to the greatest heights of success and achievement. A tremendous amount of effort was put into this book to deliver outstanding value and content to our readers, so please let your own voice be heard in the comments section of our Amazon product page.

If you enjoyed this book it would help us a lot if you would leave an honest review on Amazon. Knowing that you found this book useful will inspire us to create futher titles. Thanks again for your purchase.

Kindest Regards,

Matthew North
Editor

Quote Foundry

If you think you can do a thing or think you can't do a thing, you're right.

Henry Ford

A genuine leader is not a searcher for consensus but a molder of consensus.

Martin Luther King, Jr.

It is better to lead from behind and to put others in front, especially when you celebrate victory when nice things occur. You take the front line when there is danger. Then people will appreciate your leadership.

Nelson Mandela

A leader is best when people barely know he exists, when his work is done, his aim fulfilled, they will say we did it ourselves.

Lao Tzu

Leadership is solving problems. The day soldiers stop bringing you their problems is the day you have stopped leading them. They have either lost confidence that you can help or concluded you do not care. Either case is a failure of leadership.

Colin Powell

Effective leadership is not about making speeches or being liked; leadership is defined by results not attributes.

Peter Drucker

I suppose at one time leadership meant muscles but today it means getting along with people.

Mahatma Gandhi

Be a yardstick of quality. Some people aren't used to an environment where excellence is expected.

Steve Jobs

Be careful the environment you choose for it will shape you. Be careful of the friends you choose for you will become like them.

W. Clement Stone

Don't find fault, find a remedy.

Henry Ford

Innovation distinguishes between a leader and a follower.

Steve Jobs

When the best leader's work is done the people say, 'We did it ourselves.'

Lao Tzu

Management is doing things right, leadership is doing the right things.

Peter Drucker

Don't be afraid to give up the good to go for the great.

John D. Rockefeller

A man who wants to lead the orchestra must turn his back on the crowd.

Max Lucado

Leadership is the art of getting someone else to do something you want done because he wants to do it.

Dwight D. Eisenhower

If your actions inspire others to dream more, learn more, do more and become more, you are a leader.

John Quincy Adams

Hold yourself responsible for a higher standard than anybody expects of you. Never excuse yourself.

Henry Ward Beecher

Affirmation without discipline is the beginning of delusion.

Jim Rohn

Leadership is about taking responsibility, not making excuses.

Mitt Romney

A man always has two reasons for doing anything a good reason and the real reason.

J. P. Morgan

The cautious seldom err.

Confucius

Effective leadership is putting first things first. Effective management is discipline, carrying it out.

Stephen Covey

A leader is one who knows the way, goes the way, and shows the way.

John C. Maxwell

People ask the difference between a leader and a boss. The leader leads, and the boss drives.

Theodore Roosevelt

Give whatever you are doing and whoever you are with the gift of your attention.

Jim Rohn

A leader is a dealer in hope.

Napoleon Bonaparte

People who enjoy meetings should not be in charge of anything.

Thomas Sowell

Good leadership consists of showing average people how to do the work of superior people.

John D. Rockefeller

He who is prudent and lies in wait for an enemy who is not, will be victorious.

Sun Tzu

Leadership cannot really be taught. It can only be learned.

Harold S. Geneen

If you want a quality, act as if you already had it.

William James

Enlightened leadership is spiritual if we understand spirituality not as some kind of religious dogma or ideology but as the domain of awareness where we experience values like truth, goodness, beauty, love and compassion, and also intuition, creativity, insight and focused attention.

Deepak Chopra

A good leader takes a little more than his share of the blame, and a little less than his share of the credit.

Arnold H. Glasow

Leaders must be close enough to relate to others, but far enough ahead to motivate them.

John C. Maxwell

No man will make a great leader who wants to do it all himself or get all the credit for doing it.

Andrew Carnegie

Leadership is practiced not so much in words as in attitude and in actions.

Harold S. Geneen

Good management is the art of making problems so interesting and their solutions so constructive that everyone wants to get to work and deal with them.

Paul Hawken

To succeed in business it is necessary to make others see things as you see them

Aristotle Onassis

You have to think anyway, so why not think big?

Donald Trump

Outstanding leaders go out of their way to boost the self-esteem of their personnel. If people believe in themselves, it's amazing what they can accomplish.

Sam Walton

Example is leadership.

Albert Schweitzer

The task of the leader is to get his people from where they are to where they have not been.

Henry A. Kissinger

People who don't take risks generally make about two big mistakes a year. People who do take risks generally make about two big mistakes a year.

Peter Drucker

If you care enough for a result, you will most certainly attain it.

William James

If you command wisely, you'll be obeyed cheerfully.

Thomas Fuller

High expectations are the key to everything

Sam Walton

If a window of opportunity appears, don't pull down the shade.

Tom Peters

Leadership is unlocking people's potential to become better.

Bill Bradley

Every act of conscious learning requires the willingness to suffer an injury to one's self-esteem. That is why young children, before they are aware of their own self-importance, learn so easily.

Thomas Szasz

Leadership is influence.

John C. Maxwell

Leadership is diving for a loose ball, getting the crowd involved, getting other players involved. It's being able to take it as well as dish it out. That's the only way you're going to get respect from the players.

Larry Bird

No matter how carefully you plan your goals they will never be more than pipe dreams unless you pursue them with gusto.

W. Clement Stone

How we think shows through in how we act. Attitudes are mirrors of the mind. They reflect thinking.

David Joseph Schwartz

Go as far as you can see. When you get there, you'll be able to see farther.

J. P. Morgan

A leader does not deserve the name unless he is willing occasionally to stand alone.

Henry A. Kissinger

Leadership is the capacity to translate vision into reality.

Warren G. Bennis

The art of leadership is saying no, not saying yes. It is very easy to say yes.

Tony Blair

Making good decisions is a crucial skill at every level.

Peter Drucker

People buy into the leader before they buy into the vision.

John C. Maxwell

The real leader has no need to lead - he is content to point the way.

Henry Miller

Without initiative, leaders are simply workers in positions.

Bo Bennett

There are three secrets to managing. The first secret is have patience. The second is be patient. And the third most important secret is patience.

Chuck Tanner

No person will make a great business leader who wants to do it all himself or get all the credit.

Andrew Carnegie

Luck is a dividend of sweat. The more you sweat, the luckier you get.

Ray Kroc

Everyone who's ever taken a shower has an idea. It's the person who gets out of the shower, dries off and does something about it who makes a difference.

Nolan Bushnell

The quality of a leader is reflected in the standards they set for themselves.

Ray Kroc

It is, after all, the responsibility of the expert to operate the familiar and that of the leader to transcend it.

Henry A. Kissinger

Management is about arranging and telling. Leadership is about nurturing and enhancing.

Tom Peters

In fair weather prepare for foul.

Thomas Fuller

The first man gets the oyster, the second man gets the shell.

Andrew Carnegie

Getting in touch with your true self must be your first priority.

Tom Hopkins

When your values are clear to you, making decisions becomes easier.

Roy E. Disney

The key to being a good manager is keeping the people who hate me away from those who are still undecided.

Casey Stengel

Millions saw the apple fall, but Newton was the one who asked why.

Bernard Baruch

The amount of good luck coming your way depends on your willingness to act.

Barbara Sher

The exercise of power is determined by thousands of interactions between the world of the powerful and that of the powerless, all the more so because these worlds are never divided by a sharp line, everyone has a small part of himself in both.

Vaclav Havel

The speed of the leader is the speed of the gang.

Mary Kay Ash

The secret of my success is a two word answer: know people.

Harvey S. Firestone

Doing is a quantum leap from imagining.

Barbara Sher

Time is neutral and does not change things. With courage and initiative, leaders change things.

Jesse Jackson

Leaders must encourage their organizations to dance to forms of music yet to be heard.

Warren G. Bennis

Clarity affords focus.

Thomas Leonard

The employer generally gets the employees he deserves.

J. Paul Getty

Obstacles are things a person sees when he takes his eyes off his goal.

E. Joseph Cossman

If you have ideas, you have the main asset you need, and there isn't any limit to what you can do with your business and your life. Ideas are any man's greatest asset.

Harvey S. Firestone

I look for what needs to be done. After all, that's how the universe designs itself.

R. Buckminster Fuller

Today a reader, tomorrow a leader.

Margaret Fuller

Think little goals and expect little achievements. Think big goals and win big success.

David Joseph Schwartz

My attitude is never to be satisfied, never enough, never.

Duke Ellington

Leaders grasp nettles.

David Ogilvy

You're only as good as the people you hire.

Ray Kroc

It is rare to find a business partner who is selfless. If you are lucky it happens once in a lifetime.

Michael Eisner

The great leaders have always stage-managed their effects.

Charles de Gaulle

Get the best people and train them well.

Scott McNealy

Our business in life is not to get ahead of others, but to get ahead of ourselves.

E. Joseph Cossman

Every silver lining has a cloud.

Mary Kay Ash

Good enough never is.

Debbi Fields

Great companies in the way they work, start with great leaders.

Steve Ballmer

Strong convictions precede great actions.

James Freeman Clarke

To succeed, one must be creative and persistent.

John H. Johnson

What helps people, helps business.

Leo Burnett

Problems are only opportunities in work clothes.

Henry J. Kaiser

You have to have your heart in the business and the business in your heart.

An Wang

You have no power at all if you do not exercise constant power.

Major Owens

Whatever ought to be, can be.

James Rouse

The very exercise of leadership fosters capacity for it.

Cyril Falls

The nicest thing about standards is that there are so many of them to choose from.

Ken Olsen

A good objective of leadership is to help those who are doing poorly to do well and to help those who are doing well to do even better.

Jim Rohn

Leadership and learning are indispensable to each other.

John F. Kennedy

The supreme quality for leadership is unquestionably integrity. Without it, no real success is possible, no matter whether it is on a section gang, a football field, in an army, or in an office.

Dwight D. Eisenhower

But the person who scored well on an SAT will not necessarily be the best doctor or the best lawyer or the best businessman. These tests do not measure character , creativity, perseverance.

William Julius Wilson

You learn far more from negative leadership than from positive. Because you learn how not to do it. And, therefore, you learn how to do it.

Norman Schwarzkopf

Educationists should build the capacities of the spirit of inquiry, creativity, entrepreneurial and moral leadership among students and become their role model.

Abdul Kalam

Leadership is a privilege to better the lives of others. It is not an opportunity to satisfy personal greed.

Mwai Kibaki

You don't lead by hitting people over the head - that's assault, not leadership.

Dwight D. Eisenhower

Men make history and not the other way around. In periods where there is no leadership , society stands still. Progress occurs when courageous, skillful leaders seize the opportunity to change things for the better.

Harry S. Truman

Leadership is a potent combination of strategy and character. But if you must be without one, be without the strategy.

Norman Schwarzkopf

No institution can possibly survive if it needs geniuses or supermen to manage it. It must be organized in such a way as to be able to get along under a composed of average human beings.

Peter Drucker

Leadership is the other side of the coin of loneliness, and he who is a leader must always act alone. And acting alone, accept everything alone.

Ferdinand Marcos

Management is efficiency in climbing the ladder of success. Leadership determines whether the ladder is leaning against the right wall.

Stephen Covey

Leadership is a matter of having people look at you and gain confidence, seeing how you react. If you're in control, they're in control.

Tom Landry

Leadership to me means duty, honor, country. It means character, and it means listening from time to time.

George W. Bush

A functioning, robust democracy requires a healthy educated, participatory followership, and an educated, morally grounded leadership.

Chinua Achebe

The growth and development of people is the highest calling of leadership.

Harvey S. Firestone

Leadership in today's world requires far more than a large stock of gunboats and a hard fist at the conference table.

Hubert H. Humphrey

Leadership is getting players to believe in you. If you tell a teammate you're ready to play as tough as you're able to, you'd better go out there and do it. Players will see right through a phony. And they can tell when you're not giving it all you've got.

Larry Bird

Leadership is an opportunity to serve. It is not a trumpet call to self-importance.

J. Donald Walters

All of the great leaders have had one characteristic in common: it was the willingness to confront unequivocally the major anxiety of their people in their time. This, and not much else, is the essence of leadership.

John Kenneth Galbraith

Leadership can not be measured in a poll or even in the result of an election. It can only be truly seen with the benefit of time. From the perspective of 20 years, not 20 days.

Marco Rubio

The function of leadership is to produce more leaders, not more followers.

Ralph Nader

The secret to success is good leadership, and good leadership is all about making the lives of your team members or workers better.

Tony Dungy

Leading a team consists not in degrees of technique but in traits of character. It requires moral leadership rather than athletic or intellectual effort, and it imposes on both leader and follower alike the burdens of self-restraint.

Lewis H. Lapham

Leadership is getting someone to do what they don't want to do, to achieve what they want to achieve.

Tom Landry

I think we need the feminine qualities of leadership, which include attention to aesthetics and the environment, nurturing, affection, intuition and the qualities that make people feel safe and cared for.

Deepak Chopra

One of the tests of leadership is the ability to recognize a problem before it becomes an emergency.

Arnold H. Glasow

We live in a society obsessed with public opinion. But leadership has never been about popularity.

Marco Rubio

I forgot to shake hands and be friendly. It was an important lesson about leadership.

Lee Iacocca

To have long term success as a coach or in any position of leadership, you have to be obsessed in some way.

Pat Riley

A leader has a harder job to do than just choosing sides. It must bring sides together.

Jesse Jackson

Character matters; leadership descends from character.

Rush Limbaugh

My philosophy of leadership is to surround myself with good people who have ability, judgment and knowledge, but above all, a passion for service.

Sonny Perdue

Don't necessarily avoid sharp edges. Occasionally they are necessary to leadership.

Donald Rumsfeld

The key to successful leadership today is influence, not authority.

Ken Blanchard

Charlatanism of some degree is indispensable to effective leadership.

Eric Hoffer

Absolute identity with one's cause is the first and great condition of successful leadership.

Woodrow Wilson

Honor bespeaks worth. Confidence begets trust. Service brings satisfaction. Cooperation proves the quality of leadership .

James Cash Penney

Presidential leadership needn't always cost money. Look for low- and no-cost options. They can be surprisingly effective.

Donald Rumsfeld

Humility is a great quality of leadership which derives respect and not just fear or hatred.

Yousef Munayyer

A leader is one who, out of madness or goodness, volunteers to take upon himself the woe of the people. There are few men so foolish, hence the erratic quality of leadership in the world.

John Updike

Leadership can't be fabricated. If it is fabricated and rehearsed, you can't fool the guys in the locker room. So when you talk about leadership , it comes with performance. Leadership comes with consistency.

Junior Seau

If you don't understand that you work for your mislabeled 'subordinates,' then you know nothing of leadership. You know only tyranny.

Dee Hock

Overall, the challenge of leadership is both moral and one of developing the characteristics that make us respected by one another.

Louis Farrakhan

The task of leadership is not to put greatness into humanity, but to elicit it, for the greatness is already there.

John Buchan

In order to cultivate a set of leaders with legitimacy in the eyes of the citizenry, it is necessary that the path to leadership be visibly open to talented and qualified individuals of every race and ethnicity.

Sandra Day O'Connor

But I do not believe that the world would be entirely different if there were more women leaders. Maybe if everybody in leadership was a woman, you might not get into the conflicts in the first place.

But if you watch the women who have made it to the top, they haven't exactly been non-aggressive - including me.

Madeleine Albright

There are many elements to a campaign. Leadership is number one. Everything else is number two.

Bertolt Brecht

Leadership does not depend on being right.

Ivan Illich

Leadership is hard to define and good leadership even harder. But if you can get people to follow you to the ends of the earth, you are a great leader.

Indra Nooyi

The signs of outstanding leadership appear primarily among the followers. Are the followers reaching their potential? Are they learning? Serving? Do they achieve the required results? Do they change with grace? Manage conflict?

Max de Pree

The only safe ship in a storm is leadership.

Faye Wattleton

Leadership comes in small acts as well as bold strokes.

Carly Fiorina

If a guy is intimidated by a woman in leadership , he has real problems with his own concepts of masculinity. That's a harsh statement, but I believe it to be true.

Tony Campolo

The more that social democracy develops, grows, and becomes stronger, the more the enlightened masses of workers will take their own destinies, the leadership of their movement, and the determination of its direction into their own hands.

Rosa Luxemburg

I am endlessly fascinated that playing football is considered a training ground for leadership, but raising children isn't. Hey, it made me a better leader you have to take a lot of people's needs into account you have to look down the road. Trying to negotiate getting a couple of kids to watch the same TV show requires serious diplomacy.

Dee Dee Myers

I believe that the capacity that any organisation needs is for leadership to appear anywhere it is needed, leadership when it is needed.

Margaret J. Wheatley

I think it is quite dangerous for an organisation to think they can predict where they are going to need leadership . It needs to be something that people are willing to assume if it feels relevant, given the context of any situation.

Margaret J. Wheatley

I think a major act of leadership right now, call it a radical act, is to create the places and processes so people can actually learn together, using our experiences.

Margaret J. Wheatley

Most people associate command and control leadership with the military.

Margaret J. Wheatley

The cardinal responsibility of leadership is to identify the dominant contradiction at each point of the historical process and to work out a central line to resolve it.

Mao Zedong

Leadership cannot just go along to get along. Leadership must meet the moral challenge of the day.

Jesse Jackson

Leadership is intangible, and therefore no weapon ever designed can replace it.

Omar N. Bradley

I think one of the keys to leadership is recognizing that everybody has gifts and talents. A good leader will learn how to harness those gifts toward the same goal.

Benjamin Carson

Leadership is, among other things, the ability to inflict pain and get away with it - short-term pain for long-term gain.

George Will

Leadership is an ever-evolving position.

Mike Krzyzewski

True leadership lies in guiding others to success. In ensuring that everyone is performing at their best, doing the work they are pledged to do and doing it well.

Bill Owens

If we are to negotiate the coming years safely, we may need a new kind of leadership . To put it more precisely, we need the rediscovery of an ancient kind of that has rarely been given the prominence it deserves. I mean the leader as teacher.

Jonathan Sacks

Leadership is about being a servant first.

Allen West

The most dangerous myth is that leaders are born-that there is a genetic factor to leadership . This myth asserts that people simply either have certain charismatic qualities or not. That's nonsense in fact, the opposite is true. Leaders are made rather than born.

Warren G. Bennis

Leadership that exploits and sacrifices young people on the altar of its goals is nothing more than raw, demonic power. Genuine leadership is found in ceaseless efforts to foster young people, to pave the way forward for them.

Daisaku Ikeda

Where there is an absence of international political leadership , civil society should step in to fill the gap, providing the energy and vision needed to move the world in a new and better direction.

Daisaku Ikeda

The role of leadership is to transform the complex situation into small pieces and prioritize them.

Carlos Ghosn

Ninety percent of leadership is the ability to communicate something people want.

Dianne Feinstein

One simple way to keep organizations from becoming cancerous might be to rotate all jobs on a regular, frequent and mandatory basis, including the positions.

Robert Shea

Market leadership can translate directly to higher revenue, higher profitability, greater capital velocity, and correspondingly stronger returns on invested capital.

Jeff Bezos

Leadership involves finding a parade and getting in front of it.

John Naisbitt

If there is such a thing as good leadership, it is to give a good example. I have to do so for all the Ikea employees.

Ingvar Kamprad

Education is the mother of leadership.

Wendell Willkie

It is the responsibility of leadership to provide opportunity, and the responsibility of individuals to contribute.

William Pollard

The art of communication is the language of leadership.

James Humes

Real leadership is leaders recognizing that they serve the people that they lead.

Pete Hoekstra

China and India will take the global on climate change they are suffering for it.

Malcolm Turnbull

This is easy to say with the benefit of hindsight, but I think it once again points out how very important style of leadership , that is the way he does what he does, is to his perception.

Robert Teeter

I know of no single formula for success. But over the years I have observed that some attributes of leadership are universal and are often about finding ways of encouraging people to combine their efforts, their talents, their insights, their enthusiasm and their inspiration to work together.

Queen Elizabeth II

Being a CEO still means sitting across the table from big institutional investors and showing your leadership and having them believe in you.

Christie Hefner

We in the press, by our power, can actually undermine leadership.

Christiane Amanpour

I wish I had played team sports. I think every kid should. Teamwork builds character - teaches people about leadership and cooperation.

Mo Rocca

One secret of leadership is that the mind of a leader never turns off. Leaders even when they are sightseers or spectators, are active not passive observers.

James Humes

The more consistent a father can be or a mentor can be in the person's life and teach them principles of real solid manhood, character, integrity and leadership, the more consistent you can be in the person's life and teach them those things at a younger age, and then the better off they'll be.

Allan Houston

If people want to compete for leadership of a religious group, they can compete in piety. A chilling thought. Or funny.

Mary Douglas

Sometimes leadership is planting trees under whose shade you'll never sit. It may not happen fully till after I'm gone. But I know that the steps we're taking are the right steps.

Jennifer M. Granholm

What nourishes us at home and in school is what inspires us. When we get awareness and learn about the great potential that we all human beings have, we are able to discover our leadership.

Vicente Fox

Leadershiprequires the courage to make decisions that will benefit the next generation.

Alan Autry

An old African leader says about leadership , he says that leadership should never be shared it should always remain in the hands of the dispossessed people. We will lead the revolution.

H. Rap Brown

Divorced from ethics, leadership is reduced to management and politics to mere technique.

James MacGregor Burns

Leadership should be born out of the understanding of the needs of those who would be affected by it.

Marian Anderson

As for leadership , I am the kind who leads reluctantly and more by example than anything else. Someone had to be on the incorporation papers as president.

Keith Henson

Turnaround or growth, it's getting your people focused on the goal that is still the job of leadership.

Anne M. Mulcahy

Not everybody is created equal, and it's important for companies to identify those high potentials and treat them differently, accelerate their development and pay them more. That process is so incredibly important to developing first-class leadership in a company.

Anne M. Mulcahy

Every time you have to speak, you are auditioning for leadership.

James Humes

And I'd say one of the great lessons I've learned over the past couple of decades, from a management perspective, is that really when you come down to it, it really is all about people and all about leadership.

Steve Case

I think the greater responsibility, in terms of morality, is where leadership begins.

Norman Lear

In the area we're discussing, leadership begins on Madison Avenue, on the desks and in the offices of people who spend hundreds of millions of dollars buying what will get them ratings.

Norman Lear

In this nation, leadership is dollars.

Norman Lear

Leadership must be likeable, affable, cordial, and above all emotional. The fashion of authoritarian is gone. Football is about life. You can't be angry all day.

Vicente del Bosque

Alliances and international organizations should be understood as opportunities for leadership and a means to expand our influence, not as constraints on our power.

Chuck Hagel

But the ability to articulate what you are doing, to be clear about it, and to stick to it is, I think, the essence of political leadership.

Chris Patten

Leadership is the key to 99 percent of all successful efforts.

Erskine Bowles

Well, I think that leadership - I think 's always been about two main things: imagination and courage.

Paul Keating

Different times need different types of leadership.

Park Geun-hye

Leadership is about doing what you know is right - even when a growing din of voices around you is trying to convince you to accept what you know to be wrong.

Robert. L. Ehrlich

Actions, not words, are the ultimate results of leadership.

Bill Owens

Leadership is an active role; 'Lead' is a verb. But the leader who tries to do it all is headed for burnout, and in a powerful hurry.

Bill Owens

Leadership offers an opportunity to make a difference in someone's life, no matter what the project.

Bill Owens

Leadership demands that we make tough choices.

Alan Autry

What I've really learned over time is that optimism is a very, very important part of leadership.

Bob Iger

I think it is important for people who are given leadership roles to assume that role immediately.

Bob Iger

Leadership is working with goals and vision management is working with objectives.

Russel Honore

Leadership means forming a team and working toward common objectives that are tied to time, metrics, and resources.

Russel Honore

Music is all about leadership and there ain't really a lot of leaders.

Young Jeezy

I believe that the will of the people is resolved by a strong leadership. Even in a democratic society, events depend on a strong leadership with a strong power of persuasion, and not on the opinion of the masses.

Yitzhak Shamir

The world is starving for original and decisive leadership.

Bryant McGill

People look for their leadership to lead.

Mick Cornett

The one thing I have learned as a CEO is that leadership at various levels is vastly different. When I was leading a function or a business, there were certain demands and requirements to be a leader. As you move up the organization, the requirements for leading that organization don't grow vertically; they grow exponentially.

Indra Nooyi

That is what leadership is all about: staking your ground ahead of where opinion is and convincing people, not simply following the popular opinion of the moment.

Doris Kearns Goodwin

Because management deals mostly with the status quo and deals mostly with change, in the next century we are going to have to try to become much more skilled at creating leaders.

John P. Kotter

History has shown that one cannot legislate a culture of integrity. And yet, one of the paramount responsibilities and challenges of corporate leadership is to ensure such a culture.

Preet Bharara

Life isn't easy, and leadership is harder still.

Walter Russell Mead

In the military, I learned that leadership means raising your hand and volunteering for the tough, important assignments.

Tulsi Gabbard

I think that my leadership style is to get people to fear staying in place, to fear not changing.

Lou Gerstner

I think leadership is service and there is power in that giving to help people, to inspire and motivate them to reach their fullest potential.

Denise Morrison

Leadership is simply the ability of an individual to coalesce the efforts of other individuals toward achieving common goals. It boils down to looking after your people and ensuring that, from top to bottom, everyone feels part of the team.

Frederick Smith

The test of leadership is not to put greatness into humanity, but to elicit it, for the greatness is already there.

James Buchanan

As a woman, my style defines my leadership. It's a gentler, more compassionate approach. I consult, I listen and I compromise where it's in the best interest of the citizens.

Kamla Persad-Bissessar

It's very important in a leadership role not to place your ego at the foreground and not to judge everything in relationship to how your ego is fed.

Ruth J. Simmons

I have spent a lifetime watching kids make mistakes because they were not trained or well led or properly motivated to do well. I never faulted the kids rather, I saw opportunity to train, to motivate, to improve - not to punish the individual.

Eric Shinseki

Sport fosters many things that are good teamwork and leadership.

Daley Thompson

You have to enable and empower people to make decisions independent of you. As I've learned, each person on a team is an extension of your leadership; if they feel empowered by you they will magnify your power to lead.

Tom Ridge

Woodrow Wilson called for leaders who, by boldly interpreting the nation's conscience, could lift a people out of their everyday selves. That people can be lifted into their better selves is the secret of transforming leadership.

James MacGregor Burns

Leaders of the future will have to be visionary and be able to bring people in - real communicators. These are things that women bring to leadership and executive positions, and it's going to be incredibly valuable and incredibly in demand.

Anita Borg

Real leadership means tackling tough problems ourselves and not leaving them to our children.

Jon Kyl

Leadership appears to be the art of getting others to want to do something you are convinced should be done.

Vance Packard

Once it gets to a point where it becomes a matter of life and death to occupy a position of leadership or not, with an eye on future opportunities, therein lies the danger.

Kgalema Motlanthe

The leader is one who mobilizes others toward a goal shared by leaders and followers... Leaders, followers and goals make up the three equally necessary supports for leadershi .

Gary Wills

Leadership - mobilization toward a common goal.

Gary Wills

Leadership is particularly necessary to ensure ready acceptance of the unfamiliar and that which is contrary to tradition.

Cyril Falls

Organizations endure, however, in proportion to the breadth of the morality by which they are governed. Thus the endurance of organization depends upon the quality of leadership and that quality derives from the breadth of the morality upon which it rests.

Chester Irving Barnard

Leadership must be established from the top down.

Sam Nunn

When a man assumes leadership , he forfeits the right to mercy.

Gennaro Angiulo

To handle yourself, use your head; to handle others, use your heart.

Eleanor Roosevelt

The mediocre teacher tells. The good teacher explains. The superior teacher demonstrates. The great teacher inspires.

William Arthur Ward

It's hard to lead a cavalry charge if you think you look funny on a horse.

Adlai E. Stevenson II

Our chief want is someone who will inspire us to be what we know we could be.

Ralph Waldo Emerson

Keep your fears to yourself, but share your courage with others.

Robert Louis Stevenson

The greatest leader is not necessarily the one who does the greatest things. He is the one that gets the people to do the greatest things.

Ronald Reagan

Only one man in a thousand is a leader of men--the other 999 follow women.

Groucho Marx

Don't waste your energy trying to educate or change opinions; go over, under, through, and opinions will change organically when you're the boss. Or they won't. Who cares? Do your thing, and don't care if they like it.

Tina Fey

Power isn't control at all--power is strength, and giving that strength to others. A leader isn't someone who forces others to make him stronger; a leader is someone willing to give his strength to others that they may have the strength to stand on their own.

Beth Revis

I have three precious things which I hold fast and prize. The first is gentleness; the second is frugality; the third is humility, which keeps me from putting myself before others. Be gentle and you can be bold; be frugal and you can be liberal; avoid putting yourself before others and you can become a leader among men.

Lao Tzu

Victory has a hundred fathers and defeat is an orphan.

John F. Kennedy

You are not here merely to make a living. You are here in order to enable the world to live more amply, with greater vision, with a finer spirit of hope and achievement. You are here to enrich the world, and you impoverish yourself if you forget the errand.

Woodrow Wilson

Example is not the main thing in influencing others. It is the only thing.

Albert Schweitzer

Leaders must be close enough to relate to others, but far enough ahead to motivate them.

John C. Maxwell

The mark of a great man is one who knows when to set aside the important things in order to accomplish the vital ones.

Brandon Sanderson

Leadership is not about titles, positions, or flowcharts. It is about one life influencing another.

John C. Maxwell

You have to be burning with an idea, or a problem, or a wrong that you want to right. If you're not passionate enough from the start, you'll never stick it out.

Steve Jobs

A leader... is like a shepherd. He stays behind the flock, letting the most nimble go out ahead, whereupon the others follow, not realising that all along they are being directed from behind.

Nelson Mandela

Being responsible sometimes means pissing people off.

Colin Powell

Do you know that one of the great problems of our age is that we are governed by people who care more about feelings than they do about thoughts and ideas.

Margaret Thatcher

A leader is a dealer in hope.

Napoleon

The best executive is the one who has sense enough to pick good men to do what he wants done, and self-restraint to keep from meddling with them while they do it.

Theodore Roosevelt

I don't see myself being special; I just see myself having more responsibilities than the next man. People look to me to do things for them, to have answers.

Tupac Shakur

If you would convince a man that he does wrong, do right. But do not care to convince him. Men will believe what they see. Let them see.

Henry David Thoreau

I cannot trust a man to control others who cannot control himself.

Robert E. Lee

Consensus: The process of abandoning all beliefs, principles, values, and policies in search of something in which no one believes, but to which no one objects; the process of avoiding the very issues that have to be solved, merely because you cannot get agreement on the way ahead. What great cause would have been fought and won under the banner: 'I stand for consensus?'

Margaret Thatcher

You get in life what you have the courage to ask for.

Nancy D. Solomon

In the end, it is important to remember that we cannot become what we need to be by remaining what we are.

Max De Pree

We're here for a reason. I believe a bit of the reason is to throw little torches out to lead people through the dark.

Whoopi Goldberg

A leader isn't someone who forces others to make him stronger; a leader is someone willing to give his strength to others so that they may have the strength to stand on their own.

Beth Revis

Always remember, Son, the best boss is the one who bosses the least. Whether it's cattle, or horses, or men; the least government is the best government.

Ralph Moody

If you really want the key to success, start by doing the opposite of what everyone else is doing.

Brad Szollose

Give as few orders as possible, his father had told him once long ago. Once you've given orders on a subject, you must always give orders on that subject.

Frank Herbert

Wisdom equals knowledge plus courage. You have to not only know what to do and when to do it, but you have to also be brave enough to follow through.

Jarod Kintz

In a battle between two ideas, the best one doesn't necessarily win. No, the idea that wins is the one with the most fearless heretic behind it.

Seth Godin

If you want to build a ship, don't drum up the men to gather wood, divide the work, and give orders. Instead, teach them to yearn for the vast and endless sea.

Antoine de Saint-Exupery

Remember teamwork begins by building trust. And the only way to do that is to overcome our need for invulnerability.

Patrick Lencioni

No guts, no story.

Chris Brady

Leadership is an action, not a position.

Donald McGannon

Surround yourself with great people; delegate authority; get out of the way.

Ronald Reagan

I cannot give you a formula for success, but I can give you the formula for failure, which is: try to please everybody.

Herbert Bayard Swope

Show me the man you honor and I will know what kind of man you are.

Thomas John Carlisle

The challenge of leadership is to be strong but not rude; be kind, but not weak; be bold, but not a bully; be humble, but not timid; be proud, but not arrogant; have humor, but without folly.

Jim Rohn

If you spend your life trying to be good at everything, you will never be great at anything.

Tom Rath

Average leaders raise the bar on themselves; good leaders raise the bar for others; great leaders inspire others to raise their own bar.

Orrin Woodward

Don't blow off another's candle for it won't make yours shine brighter.

Jaachynma N.E. Agu

Whenever you see a successful business, someone once made a courageous decision.

Peter F. Drucker

When you put together deep knowledge about a subject that intensely matters to you, charisma happens. You gain courage to share your passion, and when you do that, folks follow.

Jerry Porras

A good leader leads the people from above them. A great leader leads the people from within them.

M.D. Arnold

The ultimate measure of a man is not where he stands in moments of comfort, but where he stands at times of challenge and controversy.

Martin Luther King, Jr.

It is absolutely necessary...for me to have persons that can think for me, as well as execute orders.

George Washington

When eagles are silent, parrots begin to chatter.

Winston Churchill

You don't lead by pointing and telling people some place to go. You lead by going to that place and making a case.

Ken Kesey

Become the kind of leader that people would follow voluntarily; even if you had no title or position.

Brian Tracy

I start with the premise that the function of leadership is to produce more leaders, not more followers.

Ralph Nader

Anyone can hold the helm when the sea is calm.

Publilius Syrus

A great person attracts great people and knows how to hold them together.

Johann Wolfgang Von Goethe

My job is not to be easy on people. My job is to take these great people we have and to push them and make them even better.

Steve Jobs

People buy into the leader before they buy into the vision.

John Maxwell

To have long-term success as a coach or in any position of leadership, you have to be obsessed in some way.

Pat Riley

A good plan violently executed now is better than a perfect plan executed next week.

George Patton

Earn your leadership every day.

Michael Jordan

The most effective way to do it, is to do it.

Amelia Earhart

Done is better than perfect.

Sheryl Sandberg

What you do has far greater impact than what you say.

Steven Covey

Keep your fears to yourself, but share your courage with others.

Robert Louis Stevenson

Forget about the fast lane. If you really want to fly, just harness your power to your passion.

Oprah Winfrey

Efficiency is doing the thing right. Effectiveness is doing the right thing.

Peter Drucker

There are two ways of spreading light: to be the candle or the mirror that reflects it.

Edith Wharton

Tend to the people, and they will tend to the business.

John Maxwell

The question isn't who's going to let me; it's who is going to stop me.

Ayn Rand

Outstanding leaders go out of their way to boost the self-esteem of their personnel. If people believe in themselves, it's amazing what they can accomplish.

Sam Walton

As a leader, I am tough on myself and I raise the standard for everybody; however, I am very caring because I want people to excel at what they are doing so that they can aspire to be me in the future.

Indra Nooyi

Leadership is the art of giving people a platform for spreading ideas that work.

Seth Godin

The first responsibility of a leader is to define reality. The last is to say thank you. In between, the leader is a servant.

Max DePree

To add value to others, one must first value others.

John Maxwell

A company is stronger if it is bound by love rather than by fear.

Herb Kelleher

In theory, there is no difference between theory and practice. But, in practice, there is.

Yogi Berra

Nothing can stop the man with the right mental attitude from achieving his goal; nothing on earth can help the man with the wrong mental attitude.

Thomas Jefferson

Those who let things happen usually lose to those who make things happen.

Dave Weinbaum

Success is not final, failure is not fatal: it is the courage to continue that counts.

Winston Churchill

In a moment of decision, the best thing you can do is the right thing. The worst thing you can do is nothing.

Theodore Roosevelt

When people talk, listen completely. Most people never listen.

Ernest Hemingway

The most basic of all human needs is the need to understand and be understood. The best way to understand people is to listen to them.

Ralph Nichols

Do not follow where the path may lead.

Go instead where there is no path and leave a trail.

Harold R. McAlindon

In times of change, learners inherit the Earth, while the learned find themselves beautifully equipped to deal with a world that no longer exists.

Eric Hoffer

The price of greatness is responsibility.

Winston Churchill

I must follow the people. Am I not their leader?

Benjamin Disraeli

Leadership and learning are indispensable to each other.

John F. Kennedy

The final test of a leader is that he leaves behind him in other men, the conviction and the will to carry on.

Walter Lippman

High sentiments always win in the end, The leaders who offer blood, toil, tears and sweat always get more out of their followers than those who offer safety and a good time. When it comes to the pinch, human beings are heroic.

George Orwell

Our chief want is someone who will inspire us to be what we know we could be.

Ralph Waldo Emerson

I think leadership comes from integrity – that you do whatever you ask others to do. I think there are non-obvious ways to lead. Just by providing a good example as a parent, a friend, a neighbour makes it possible for other people to see better ways to do things. Leadership does not need to be a dramatic, fist in the air and trumpets blaring, activity.

Scott Berkun

The leaders who work most effectively, it seems to me, never say I. And that's not because they have trained themselves not to say I. They don't think I. They think we; they think team. They understand their job to be to make the team function. They accept responsibility and don't sidestep it, but we gets the credit.... This is what creates trust, what enables you to get the task done.

Peter Drucker

Innovation distinguishes between a leader and a follower.

Steve Jobs

As we look ahead into the next century, leaders will be those who empower others.

Bill Gates

It is impossible to imagine anything which better becomes a ruler than mercy.

Seneca

Never doubt that a small group of thoughtful, concerned citizens can change world. Indeed it is the only thing that ever has.

Margaret Mead

Thank you

Thanks again for your purchase on Kindle. I would greatly appreciate it if you would kindly leave an honest review on our Kindle product page.

To your success,

Matthew North
Editor

Quote Foundry